To Explore Strategy

探索戰略

Bilingual Edition(中英雙語版)

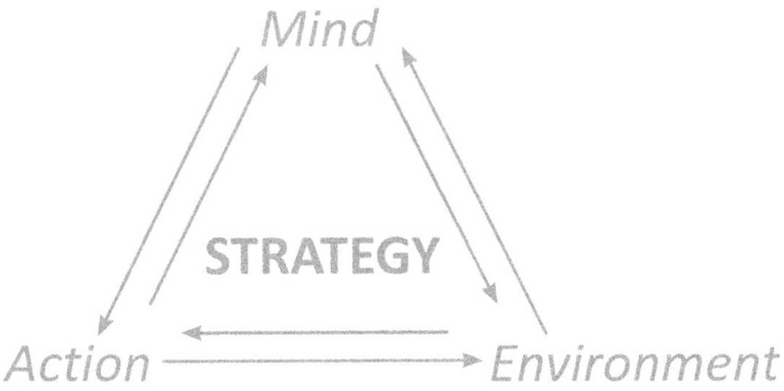

By Chong Han Wang
王崇翰 著

Copyright

Book: To Explore Strategy (Bilingual Edition)
Author: Chong Han Wang
Published by Chong Han Wang

No.400, Sec.4, Qinghai Rd., Taitung City, Taitung County, Taiwan(950)
Email: worldjody@gmail.com

First Published : 2016

The catalog record of this book is available from the National Central Library (Taiwan).

ISBN 978-957-43-3955-6 Paperback
ISBN 978-957-43-3976-1 Ebook

Contents
（目錄）

English Version

Chinese Version
（中文版本）

Chapter 1

To Find The Elements of Strategy

Being a conceptual product, strategy arises from that human beings endeavor to understand the world and attempt to realize their wishes in the world. Humans have applied strategy to all kinds of problems and purposes, such as political decisions, economic development, military conflicts, environmental protection, social issues, and technological innovation.

However, there is no solid consensus on strategy's fundamental characteristic. Although humans have developed many definitions about strategy, these definitions are not unified. Ideas are designed for human purposes; different purposes develop different ideas. So strategy has been developed into many versions for different human purposes, and these versions' concepts about strategy are varied.

A curious question is how strategy could be developed into different versions. A feasible answer is that strategy is a structure composed of several elements which could be easily adjusted to various situations for different purposes. In other words, some elements build up strategy and could flexibly modify themselves to change strategy into different versions for different situations.

If the elements are found, strategy could be learned better. A viable way of searching the elements is to discover the same factors that all versions of strategy face in tackling any situation for their goals. If certain same factors really constitute any situation, every version of strategy develops similar ideas centered around the factors. As a result, the factors become the needful elements of strategy's ideas, for confronting any situation. In other words, the factors are the elements of strategy.

SEARCHING FOR THE SAME FACTORS CONSTITUTING ANY SITUATION

The process of searching the same factors among all situations starts from investigating what fundamentally causes any situation because the thing that fundamentally causes a situation is the requisite factor constituting the situation.

Except for natural phenomena, in human society, every situation is caused by people's action. Any action of people has practical effects on the world and builds relations between different factors. Action uses the effects and the relations to develop a situation.

For example, a country's government invests more money in universities to train more professionals in order to boost the national economy. The governmental action's direct effect is universities could strengthen educational ability to train more skilled people with extra financial support; the indirect effect is the increase of skilled people might help the country's economy. Meanwhile, the government's action builds relations between four different factors: political factor (the investment of national fund); educational factor (the training capacity of universities); social factor (the number of professionals in the country); economic factor (the country's economic development). The action of the government uses these effects and the relations between the four factors to develop a situation : the improvement of the national economy.

Without action, every situation in human society could not happen. Only via action, different factors could be combined together to create a situation. Thus, action is an essential factor to constitute any situation in human society.

In addition to action, another essential factor is the human mind. The mind decides action: what action should be taken and how to carry out the action are governed by the psychological mechanism of the mind. Without the mind's decision, action would not appear, and any situation could not happen as a result. In addition, what and how the mind thinks affect the selection and implementation of action; so the thinking of the mind could shape a situation's development via action. Thus, the mind could cause and affect any situation's development. The mind is the second essential factor constituting any situation.

Moreover, any situation happens in a certain environment; any situation definitely has connections with its environment. An environment affects any situation in it via people's action: during the implementation of action in an environment, many environmental factors could affect the action, so the result of the implementation might get changed and the situation caused by the action would be different. For example, a region's geographic and climatic characteristics influence the efficiency of military action, so the result of battle might be changed by a region's natural environment.

Any situation is not only indirectly affected by its environment via people's action, it is also directly affected by its environment. When a situation happens in an environment, the situation gets integrated into the environment and interacts with the environment's factors. During the interaction, the situation is gradually changed by these environmental factors. For example, the political and economic factors of a country impact on the country's social situation; wrong governmental policy and negative economic growth worsen the unemployment rate of a country and impact the quality of civilians' lives; in other words, the political and economic environment affects the social situation.

Thus, no matter which type of environment a situation faces, any situation's development is influenced by its environment directly or indirectly; an environment becomes the essential factor constituting a situation.

IN CONCLUSION

The mind, action, and a certain environment are the three indispensable factors to constitute any situation so that strategy has to confront the three factors all the time. Thus, strategy develops its ideas around the three factors, these factors become the vital pillars to build any strategic thought. Consequently, the three factors turn into integral elements of strategy.

Chapter 2

The Essence of Strategy

The mind, action, and environment are the fundamental elements of strategy. The three elements basically constitute strategy so that the essence of strategy has strong connections with the three elements. If these elements could be understood well, strategy could be learned better.

THE MIND

The Mind For Thinking

By nature, the mind is designed to think, where every thought is constructed and processed. What composes the mind is the ingredient of producing thoughts and is also the factor affecting the process of constructing thoughts. For instance, experience, perception, knowledge, value, cognition, and emotion are the essential components constituting the mind; the components build the psychological nature of any person. These psychological components are the origin of thinking: they are used by the mind as meaningful ingredients for constructing ideas. In addition, these components are also the basic materials to build up the spiritual structure of the mind which shapes the way of constructing ideas.

The Mental Ability To Consider Environments

One crucial thinking capability of the mind is to study environments, especially the one relevant to people's action or lives. The mind searches and analyzes numerous phenomena or meaningful clues from an environment in order to understand it. The further purpose of understanding an environment is to estimate the relation between this environment and people, with learning how people have been affected by it, how people have interacted with it, what they are able to do within it, and how this environment could possibly affect them. Once the mind clearly realizes the relation, it would think if it is satisfied with the relation; then the mind would consider adjusting the relation by influencing this environment based on its expectations.

During the process of thinking about an environment, the

factual information about this environment is not the only thing considered by the mind, the psychological components of the mind are also involved in the thinking. So the mind's psychological components have an impact on people's understanding and judgement about an environment. Humans' understanding and judgement about an environment influence the way of people's interaction with it; the understanding and judgement directly affect people's action and indirectly affect this environment via the action.

The Mental Ability To Make Decision

Another thinking capability of the mind is to decide. People desire to accomplish all of what they want. However, with limited vigour, time, and resource, people could only try to attain few of their wishes. Accordingly, making sure what they want to achieve as priority is vital. A person's mind prioritizes all desires of the person, chooses one of them as the most important goal, and decides what action or plan to carry out the goal, by weighing the psychological components of the person, environmental information, and other kinds of factors. Thus, decision making of humans is governed by the mind and is affected by the mind's psychological components. In addition, the decision of the mind is set as a spiritual sign that guides how people act in the future.

ACTION

Action's Interrelation With The Mind

Action does not happen automatically without a purpose, it is activated intentionally. Action is considered, selected, and utilized by the thinking process of the mind for human purposes. As a result, what action is chosen and how it could be taken place are related to the way of thinking of people.

Meanwhile, any action by people has an impact on the mind. The experience of implementing action forms a feedback to stimulate the mind. The mind reviews its thoughts and adjusts its way of thinking with referring to the experience of implementation, and the adjustment will alter the selection and implementation of action in the future.

The Important Function Of Action

Only through action, humans could actually contact different kinds of things in the world and deal with them. Action's most important function is practically influencing an environment by interacting with things of the environment, for humans' purposes. During the interaction with various things of an environment, action coordinates these things to develop a situation in the environment, based on humans' ideas and imaginations; consequently, this environment is transformed by action.

ENVIRONMENT

The Four Aspects Of Any Environment

Any environment has four aspects: material aspect, spiritual aspect, time, and space. The four aspects are the fundamental dimensions shaping every environment. All things in the world are composed of or relevant to the four aspects.

-- MATERIAL ASPECT --

Most natural things that constitute the world are physical, such as plants, terrain, ocean, and air. These natural things interact with each other according to the laws of nature. The interaction between the natural things constructs the physical characteristics of any environment: geographic condition, climatic condition, and ecological condition. An environment's physical characteristics affect all kinds of things in it.

People have to deal with the physical characteristics of any environment in order to survive and develop their lives within it. Born without anything but only with the body, humans explore and take advantage of anything in an environment to change this environment for improving living conditions and building their societies. People use accessible natural materials to invent helpful tools, technologies, and other artificial things; these human inventions strengthen people's ability to interact with and affect various things of the world. With the help of human inventions, humans could reshape many environments and develop their societies in these environments more efficiently.

In addition, many artificial things that have been produced or constructed by humans get embedded in the world as part of it and affect the world as natural things. For example, a big river in a region affects the region's ecological system. The river provides water to nurture plants and animals in the region, creating a suitable living condition for many creatures. If a big dam is built on the river, the dam would reduce the water flow of the river, and the region's ecological system is impacted.

Thus, material things, including natural ones and artificial ones, become the integral parts of the world. They fundamentally construct and significantly affect any environment. Humans endure the influence of material things but also rely on them for living and building societies. To sum up, material things fundamentally make up an important facet of every environment.

-- SPIRITUAL ASPECT --

Material things are not the only factors shaping and affecting any environment, humans are also the vital factors. Humans are guided by what and how they think. People affect the physical characteristics of an environment based on how they consider making their lives better. Some people prefer getting assimilated into the ecological system of a place without changing it to a large extent. Some people favor controlling the ecological system of an area by altering terrain and by managing plants and animals for their convenience. For the long term development of their societies, many people modify the geography of many regions by putting big artificial constructions on the land and underground on a large scale.

In addition to shaping the physical aspect of any environment, people also think about how to interact with other people. All human beings try to influence anything in the world, especially including their own kind, for their purposes; thus, any person might affect or be affected by another person. Every person could consider what action should be taken to influence other people or deal with the action of others. The thoughts of a person influence how the person takes action to interact with other people.

Taking action is not the only way to affect other people. Human beings have transformed their thoughts into varied elements of culture or society, such as language, art, law, social institutions, organizations, education, religion, tradition, social value, and etc.... When people interact with these elements and take them into account, the thoughts underlying or constructing these elements affect people's behaviors and thinking. Thus, people could influence other people psychologically, in an indirect way, on a larger scale, for a longer time, through these social and cultural elements.

No matter what human beings have done to shape this world and affect other people, the indispensable influential factors behind any action and any decision are human thoughts. Although human thoughts are invisible themselves, they truly exist in different intangible and tangible forms: thoughts are stored in the mind as memory, experience, knowledge, and personality; thoughts are hidden in languages, words, symbols, and other things people have created; or thoughts are converted into different cultural or social systems. These forms could be called as spiritual forms because human thoughts are the intrinsic part of them. Thoughts often influence how people think and act via these spiritual forms, becoming the deep root of many affairs and situations in human society. So people have to take these forms and the thoughts underlying them into consideration when they confront other people and their societies. As a result, spiritual things, which include various thoughts and the forms they exist in, construct a fundamental facet of any environment.

-- TIME --

Everything happens in a certain period of time and has deep relevance to its historical time. Every period of time has its own special historical context. Anything definitely interacts with the context of its time in a certain way: something is caused by the factors related to its era; something might be the important factor having an impact on its historical period; or something and its historical context mutually influence each other.

Moreover, any environment constantly changes over time. Any environment has developed from what it was, and what it is now is transforming into what it will be. Various factors in the world will affect any environment and gradually change any environment's current situation into a different one in the future, the relation between the past situation and the present one is also the same. In other words, the past has cultivated the present, and the present is shaping the future.

Because every environment changes over time, the development of any environment's situation has continuity. Factors of the past have caused the current situation, and some of them still get embedded in the current situation to continue their influence, such as cultural values and social systems. In a similar way, factors of the present will shape the future situation, and their influence will last into the future to some extent. So the past, the present, and the future are relevant to each other.

Thus, all things of every environment are related to time; various things in the world establish temporal connections with each other. Knowing what historical era a thing belongs to, how the thing is influenced by the context of its era and how it affects the context of its era can be studied. In addition, understanding in which historical period a situation happened, it is possible to study the relation between the situation and the one of an earlier period, and the connection between the situation and the one of a later period. Moreover, because the development of any environment's situation has continuity, human beings could estimate what an environment's situation will be based on what it is.

In short, no matter what environment a thing happens in, time is the important element to connect situations of different historical periods; time is also the crucial element that makes different things in the world linked to each other. So, time is the integral aspect of every environment.

-- SPACE --

Any environment is an actual space. Being material or non-material, everything that exists in, interacts with, or has an impact on an environment is spatially associated with it.

Spatially, how different kinds of things spread in an environment and what the relation between them is indicate how this environment is shaped. A kind of thing that scatters in the most part of an environment makes up the basic character of the environment. In case that the thing not only occurs in the most part of the environment but also overwhelms other kinds of things in terms of existence and influence, obviously the thing dominates the environment's characteristic. In another case, there are many types of things in an environment where they all prevail, but no one overpowers the others; as a result, diversity becomes the environment's typical scenery. If a certain thing only generally appears in a place of the world, it is absolutely the distinct feature of the place.

Moreover, the development of any environment's situation has relation to space. Assuming anything in an environment is not influenced by other things on the outside, the development of the environment's situation is solely linked to the environment's local factors; however, if what happens in the environment is regularly intertwined with many things existing in nearby areas, the situation of the environment is easily influenced by its adjacent places. If what happen in rather distant places often interplay with the situation in an environment, development of this environment's situation is pertinent to the factors of faraway regions to some extent.

As the situation of any environment, any factor also has relation to space. A factor able to interact with what happen in many faraway societies could exert influence on many environments cross-regionally. If another factor has interaction with innumerable kinds of things within a wider radius at the same time, it might cause situations on a large scale.

Thus, everything in the world is relevant to space, because every environment is an actual space. The development of any environment's situation, the interaction of various things, and the influence of factors cannot be completely explained without taking spatial scale into consideration. In brief, space is a crucial facet of every environment.

Environment As The Context Of Action

Any environment is the context of action's implementation; every environment provides resources that action needs. In order to affect an environment according to people's ideas, implementing action is necessary. However, the power of humans is limited so that people take advantage of what they have found in an environment to strengthen their action. For example, humans collect mineral ore of a place and transform it into a variety of metallic tools which are powerful to help modify the geographical landscape of the place. In addition, in history, with employing cultural and social systems, people in a region often organized themselves into a consolidated society against their nearby military enemy, or they established a collaborative community to build and manage grand hydraulic systems on their living place for agricultural development. No matter resources in an environment are material or spiritual, they are exploited by human beings to strengthen action to influence this environment.

Any environment is not only a place that accommodates various resources for action to use, but it is also the context that affects action. Every environment has various factors, and the interaction between these factors forms the basic characteristics of an environment, for example: climate, terrain, plant, and animal are the factors to construct the natural characteristics of an environment; meanwhile cultural values, religious tradition, social systems, economic development, political regime are the factors to shape the social characteristics of an environment. An environment's basic characteristics and factors affect action: when a type of action is implemented in an environment, the action contacts and interacts with the environment's factors; during the interaction, these factors, as well as the environment's characteristics, affect the action's implementation.

Environment As The Context Of The Mind

Any environment is not only the context of action but also the one of the mind. When gathering information about an environment, the mind could use the information to evaluate if its thoughts and way of thinking are really helpful for people to understand and interact with the environment. If the result of the evaluation is negative, the mind would readjust its thinking. In other words, an environment's situation stimulates the mind to re-estimate and readjust itself. Accordingly, any environment serving as the external context affects the internal development of the mind.

CONCLUSION

The mind, action, and environment are the fundamental elements constituting strategy; the essence of strategy is the interactive relation between these three elements. The mind is the heart of strategy which establishes the conceptual foundation of action: the mind develops thoughts to shape, sets a goal to guide, and decides a method to implement action. Action is the catalyst of strategy: action tries to make thoughts of the mind actually happen in an environment. Environment is the context of strategy, in which the mind's ideas are developed and action is carried out.

The relations between the three strategic elements are not one way, but mutual. The mind decides how and why to implement action, when action gives the experience of implementation to the mind for making the mind reconsider its decision and thinking. Action affects and changes an environment, while reversely this environment supplies resources to action and influences action's implementation. While the mind attempts to understand an environment and plans to affect it, this environment motivates the transformation of the mind's thinking.

In short, the mind, action, and environment are interrelated; the interrelationship between the three elements constructs the nature of strategy.

Chapter 3

To Understand

After studying the nature of strategy, how to employ strategy to achieve purposes is the next curious problem. However, no matter which purpose people want to achieve, they have to face an environment that is relevant to the purpose; they need to interact with this environment's situation to actualize their purpose in this environment. If the situation is learned comprehensively, a suitable plan could be designed to tackle it to increase the possibility of achieving people purpose. Thus, no matter how strategy is applied to people's goals, understanding becomes an indispensable step of strategy.

THE BASIC PRINCIPLES OF UNDERSTANDING

About understanding, there are several helpful principles which should be considered.

What Is True Depends On Truth Itself

The basic purpose of understanding is to find the truth about a situation or something. Only could people know the nature of a thing is or what actually happens, they are able to make an appropriate scheme for it.

Human beings commonly search truth via what they have learned: many ones depend on experience, knowledge, and theory to find what is true. They believe that the organized intellectual concepts really tell them what truth is and guide them to identify what is true. However, what the intellectual concepts have taught is different. These concepts just show people what a situation could be or which factors are possibly related to each other based on what have been studied.

The roles of experience, knowledge, and theory in the process of understanding are suggesting clues and stimulating people to investigate what might be connected with truth, rather than judging what truth is. Experience, knowledge, and theory could not replace truth because they are not truth itself.

The worse scenario is some people study according to their personal values. The values guide people to search what they believe is true and avoid what they believe otherwise. Accordingly, what these people learn is the information meeting the requirement of their values, instead of truth.

What is true is decided by truth itself. The basic way to understand truth is to look for and prove a thing's elemental characteristic and what actually happens, without just making a conclusion based on what have been learned or personal values.

Be Aware Of The Complexity Of the World

The real world is complex. Many situations in the world are shaped by various factors; the diversity of these factors and their relation complicate many situations. Because of the complexity, it is barely possible to take all factors into consideration. Therefore, figuring out a situation totally is difficult.

Knowing the difficulty of understanding a situation completely for its complexity, simplifying the situation becomes an alternative approach because studying the simplified situation is easier. The way of simplification is looking for the vital factors that contribute to a situation and analyzing how the situation is produced by these factors. However, the idea of simplifying a situation is sometimes misused in a way that only a few factors are selected to explain a situation. The concept of simplification is to find the real important factors that powerfully shape a situation, without taking too many irrelevant and minor factors into consideration. The purpose of simplification is to understand a situation without burdening the mind with too many details, rather than just reducing the number of factors. Oversimplification not only neglects insignificant factors but also some essential ones, reducing the possibility of basically understanding a situation.

Accordingly, being aware of the complexity of the world is necessary, while trying to understand anything. The awareness of complexity reminds people to consider that whether a situation is oversimplified as being studied.

Any Situation Changes Over Time

Any situation does not stand still forever but keeps changing over time. A situation would change a little after being studied so that it is important not to overly rely on the information which has been researched. Intelligence about any situation should keep updated.

HOW TO START UNDERSTANDING A SITUATION

To Find What And Who Are Relevant

After the discussion about the three principles, how to begin understanding a situation is the next concerning topic. Since strategy is constructed by the mind, action, and environment, the process of understanding a situation starts from the three strategic elements. The first step is to find things and people that are critically relevant to a situation in terms of the three strategic elements; what and who are relevant is defined by that if they influence a situation or they are influenced by the situation. To find what and who are relevant could begin by thinking about several questions, for example:

People and their minds

- Who significantly influences or causes a situation?
- Who is critically affected by a situation?
- Who wants to affect a situation?
- Who will influence a situation?
- Who will be influenced by a situation?

- What are the thoughts and ways of thinking of the people who influence or will influence a situation?
- How do the people affected by a situation think?

Environment

- Which kind of environment influences the development of a situation, for example: natural environment, political environment, economic environment, social environment, cultural environment, or other kinds?
- What environment is affected by a situation?
- Which kind of environment will influence a situation?
- What environment will be affected by a situation?
- Which environmental factor influences a situation, such as climatic condition, geographic condition, military conflicts, economic development, social systems, cultural value, political ideology, or other factors?
- What is the spatial scale of an environment affecting a situation?
- What geographical sphere do a situation and its influence encompass?
- What historical time has a situation undergone?
- What historical factors and historical context contributed to a situation's development?

Action

- What action causes a situation?
- What action is affected by a situation?
- What action will cause a situation?
- What action will be affected by a situation?
- What action will the people affected by a situation take to respond to the situation?

With the help of these questions, it is possible to find the relevant people and things.

To Study The Relevant People And Things

After knowing who and what are relevant, the following step is to research them. The first priority of research is studying their essence. Essence is at least made up of two kinds of components: the first kind is the basic characteristic that constitutes a thing or a person, and the characteristic dominates them all the time; the other kind is the fundamental cause that generates the basic characteristic. Thus, studying the essence of anything could firstly analyze its basic characteristic and then investigate the factor causing the characteristic. For example, a person's basic characteristic is the person's thoughts and way of thinking, because what and how the person thinks constantly influence the person's actions. One critical factor that shapes a person's thoughts and way of thinking is the person's psychological traits; the psychological components of the person's mind build up the traits.

The next priority of research is to investigate the connection between the relevant people and things. The important mission of investigation is to understand the causal relation between the relevant people and things: what or who affects which thing or which person; how the influencing one interacts with the influenced one; what is the result of their interaction?

By studying the nature of a situation's relevant things and people and the relationship between them, people could basically understand the situation: people could clearly analyze what has happened, what is happening, and how the situation has been caused.

PREDICTION

Based on the study of a situation as well as the analysis of its relevant people and things, what the situation will be or what will happen could be reasonably predicted. For example: What action will people take to change the situation? How will environmental factors transform the situation? How will the situation affect an environment?

With a profound understanding of a situation and reasonable prediction about the situation, a suitable plan could be designed to deal with it.

Chapter 4
Planning

In addition to understanding, planning is another vital process of strategy. In order to boost the odds of achieving a goal, a plan's basic function is thinking how to manage what people can do and what people can utilize to confront what has happened, what is happening, and what will happen. Implementing action randomly without thinking and preparation might squander what we have owned and ruin what we have done, putting the possibility of getting a goal at risk. That is why human beings often make plans.

There are some concepts to be discussed as helpful guides to planning.

TO CONTEMPLATE THE WHOLE CONSEQUENCE OF A PLAN

There is a common idea that achieving objectives is a good result. However, if an objective is completed with losing everything, could the result be regarded as a good one? If a plan has been realized with side-effects caused by the plan's implementation that would be harmful to the future, is the result acceptable as a good one? The answers to the two questions are definitely "not" so that reconsidering which result is good becomes necessary.

No matter what a plan is intended to pursue, the overall consequence caused by the plan is what the plan will inevitably confront: whether a plan's goal would be realized is just one part of the consequence, how the plan's implementation would affect the current situation is also included in the consequence. In addition to getting objectives, the overall consequence would be better if a plan's influence on the current situation would be beneficial or at least not too harmful. Therefore, a plan needs to take the whole consequence into account, rather than just considering its goal. The least people can do is to think what would be caused by a plan's implementation or by its action.

In short, only fulfilling a purpose is not good enough for a plan, a positive overall consequence beyond getting the purpose is more desirable.

TO THINK WHAT IS POSTIVE AND WHAT IS NEGATIVE FOR A PLAN

What Is Positive

One concept about designing a plan is to find anything that is or would be positive for the plan, in order to improve the possibility of the plan's success. With regard to this concept, thinking what is beneficial for a plan is a viable method. For example: which thought, skill, and resources are actually useful to facilitate a plan's implementation; what resources, knowledge, and other advantageous things do we have for strengthening our ability to realize a plan's objective; what environmental factors are valuable to help a plan's implementation? Finding what is beneficial for a plan would assist materializing the plan more conveniently.

Another method is to find opportunities, for instance: when is the appropriate timing to conduct an operation; which possible method could help practice a plan; is there any environmental factor or resource that has been unknown but could be exerted? Searching opportunities is to learn what would be potentially helpful for further advancing the implementation of a plan.

The third viable method is to develop what would be positive for a plan. People could create or develop what they lack if they think it would be necessary and helpful in achieving their purpose, rather than overly relying on what they have now. For example: a country could cultivate a type of industry it does not have if the industry would be beneficial for the country's economic development. To develop what would be positive is to improve the current situation for a plan. Thus, planning should not only think what the current situation is but also consider how to make it better for a plan's implementation. In addition to what people own, if they are short of certain things that will be helpful for a plan, people could develop the things for the plan.

What Is Negative

To prepare for what would hamper or endanger a plan, looking for anything that is or would be negative for the plan is another essential concept of planning. A method related to this concept is to review the limitation of a plan, for example

: how many resources are available for the plan; how much time does the plan have; what is the utmost strength of the organization that executes the plan? By understanding the limitation of a plan, what it can do and what it cannot do are clearly learned; then the plan could cautiously manage its action and resources. In addition, a plan would not overuse various things beyond their limits.

Another method is considering cost. Everything entails effort, time, or resource to some extent, for functioning well or for being developed successfully; the implementation of a plan also costs something. How much time and how many resources does a plan require? What skill and specialty are needed for a plan? Which type of action is requisite for a plan? By knowing a plan's cost as well as its limitation, what the plan is able to do and what it is unable to do could be estimated; thus, the plan could regulate its resources and action efficiently and reasonably.

In addition to learning the limitation and the cost, the other method is to study what would put a plan at risk, for instance : who would disrupt the implementation of the plan; which environmental factor could adversely affect the plan's implementation; what kind of incident could happen to hamper the execution of the plan? The purpose of studying what would endanger a plan is making preparation to neutralize or compromise any risk for the plan.

Various factors in this world affect a plan in diverse ways. Therefore, considering different factors that would influence the possibility of realizing a plan is important for planning; at least that which factors are good or bad for the plan should be investigated.

TO THINK HOLISTICALLY

In this world, different things or factors are connected by their interaction, such as the interrelation between domestic politics, international politics, military ability, economic development, and trade; they affect each other directly or indirectly via a chain reaction that an interaction between factors triggers another one. As a result, different things construct a system of interconnection, within which any member of the system could mutually influence each other. Moreover, all members together cultivate the characteristic of this system by their interaction, and the system's characteristic is totally distinct from the one of any individual member. Anything in or entering into the system would experience the influence of its characteristic and its members.

Every situation is a system that is constituted by different factors. Different factors in a situation are not independent of each other but are mutually related. Their interaction develops, maintains, and transforms the situation. In other words, a situation is established on the integrated interrelation of its factors. When a plan wants to understand any situation, the plan has to study the integrated interrelation of the situation's factors, instead of only analyzing these factors individually. Accordingly, holistic thinking is necessary for a plan to confront any situation.

In addition, a plan could be viewed in a holistic way: a plan is an organized structure, instead of an agglomeration of different ideas. If a plan is a structure, its purpose and some principles compose the core of the structure that guides the designing of the plan. Action and different ways of implementation are the main pillars to support the core, their main function is enforcing the plan's ideas to get the purpose. Managing resources as well as coordinating resources and action is the foundation of the structure, which helps the implementation of the plan. The remaining part of the plan is supportive of carrying out action, managing resources, or other main functions. Each part of a plan connects with another one, and all parts mutually support each other.

Accordingly, during planning, a plan should be regarded as an integrated system, and all things relevant to a plan are treated as a whole. All components of a plan are designed on the basis of what it wants to achieve and some guiding principles. These components are systematized to serve different functions in the plan, and they are arranged to bolster each other.

TO KEEP THE MIND ACTIVE AND SENSITIVE

Because every situation that a plan faces keeps changing over time, the mind has to be sensitive to a situation's development and actively updates the intelligence about it. Then, with reference to the renewed information, the original plan of the mind should be overhauled.

In other words, the mind should not stop thinking after creating a plan. Any plan is not perfect and would not be always appropriate, so that the mind has to be continuously aware of the current situation and what the current situation will be, for reviewing and improving its plan.

TO THINK BASED ON TRUTH

With actually understanding a situation, a plan could tackle it in a suitable way. Therefore, a plan has to base thinking on truth, instead of only on guessing and imagination. Although a plan might involve assumptions, suggestions, and predictions, these ideas have to be based on reality.

Chapter 5
To Review The Mind

In terms of strategy, no matter what action is selected, whatever thought is created, and however a plan is designed, the mind influences the thinking about these things deeply; hence reviewing the mind critically is crucial.

In the beginning, what is being thought in the mind should be clearly investigated. Then, it is needed to study which factors influence the mind's thinking as well as how the factors affect the thinking. As a result, what and how the mind thinks are approximately learned.

The next step is to test the rationality and validity of the thoughts and the way of thinking of the mind according to logic, truth, and other justified foundations. The purpose is to examine whether they are useful or harmful to researching, judging, analyzing, and planning.

The third process is to revise the mind's ideas and thinking methods.

Moreover, it is better to often seriously practice studying, analyzing, pondering, and judging various situations to improve the mind's thinking.

Strategy starts from the mind. Once humans want to understand the world and pursue their purposes, the ideas relevant to strategy arise from their minds. The ideas significantly affect thinking, planning, and plans' implementation. Thus, being aware of, evaluating, and improving what and how the mind thinks are essential.

探索戰略

-To Explore Strategy-

第一章

尋找
戰略的基本要素

作為一種概念性的產物，戰略是由於人類努力去了解這個世界並企圖在這個世界實現他們期望的事情而產生。如今，人類已經把戰略應用在各種問題和目的上，例如：政治決策、經濟發展、軍事衝突、環境保護、社會議題、以及科技創新。

然而，至今為止，人類對於戰略的根本性質還沒有一個強而有力的共識。雖然人類已經發展出許多關於戰略的定義，但這些定義並不一致。想法是為了人類目的而設計出的；不同的目的就會發展出不同的想法。所以，為了人類不同的目的，戰略被發展成許多不同的版本，而這些版本對於戰略的概念各不相同。

有趣的問題在於戰略如何能被發展成不同的版本。一個可能的答案為戰略是一個由一些要素組成的結構，為了不同的目的，這個結構可以很容易地調整以對應各種情況。

換句話說，某些要素構成戰略，而且這些要素可以彈性地調整它們自己將戰略改變成不同的版本以適應不同的情況。

如果這些要素被找到，戰略就能被更好地了解。尋找這些要素的一個可行方式就是去發現戰略的所有版本為了它們的目標在處理任何情況時都要面對的相同因素。如果特定的相同因素確實構成任何情況，戰略的每個版本就會圍繞這些因素發展出類似的想法。其結果是，為了面對任何情況，這些因素成為戰略思想不可或缺的要素。換句話說，這些因素是戰略的要素。

尋找構成任何情況的相同因素

尋找所有情況擁有的相同因素從調查什麼事物根本地造成任何情況開始，因為根本地造成一個情況的事物就是構成這個情況的必要因素。

除了自然現象，在人類社會中，每個情況都是由人類的行動造成。任何人類的行動都會對這個世界造成影響並且建立不同因素之間的關係。行動利用它所造成的影響和在不同因素間建立的關係去發展一個情況。

例如，為了提升國家經濟，一個國家的政府投資大學更多的資金去訓練更多專業人才。這個政府行動的直接影響是大學在得到額外的財務支援下可以強化教育能力以培養更多的專業人才；間接的影響是專業人才的增長可能有助於這個國家的經濟。同時，這個政府行動在四個不同因素之間建立關係：政治因素（國家資金的挹注）；教育因素（大學的訓練能力）；社會因素（國內的專業人才的數量）；經濟因素（國家的經濟發展）。這個政府的行動利用這些影響和四個因素之間的關係去發展一個情況：國家經濟的改善。

沒有行動，人類社會中的每個情況都不可能會發生。只有透過行動，不同的因素才能被結合在一起以產生一個情況。因此，在人類社會中，行動是構成任何情況的一個根本因素。

除了行動，另外一個根本因素是人類心靈。心靈決定行動：應該採取怎樣的行動以及如何實施這個行動都是由心靈的心理機制控制。沒有心靈的決定，行動不會出現，最後的結果是任何情況都無法發生。此外，心靈在思考什麼和心靈如何思考都影響行動的選擇和實施；所以心靈的思考會透過行動塑造一個情況的發展。因此心靈會造成並且影響任何情況的發展。心靈成為了構成任何情況的第二個根本因素。

此外，任何情況都發生在一個特定的環境中；任何情況必定與它自己的環境有關聯。一個環境透過人類的行動影響在它裡面的任何情況：在一個環境中實施行動的時候，許多環境因素都會影響這個行動，這個行動實施的結果可能因此改變，而這個行動所造成的情況將會有所不同。例如：一個地區的地理和氣候特性影響軍事行動的效率；所以戰鬥的結果可能被一個地區的自然環境改變。

任何情況不只經由人類行動間接地受到它自己的環境影響，也直接地受到它自己的環境影響。當一個情況發生在一個環境裡面時，這個情況會融入於這個環境並且與這個環境所包含的因素互動。在與這些因素互動的時候，這個情況會逐漸地被這些環境因素轉變。例如：一個國家的政治及經濟因素會影響這個國家的社會情況；錯誤的政府政策和經濟成長的倒退將使一個國家的失業率更糟並衝擊人民的生活品質；換句話說，政治及經濟環境影響社會情況。

因此，無論一個情況面對哪個類型的環境，任何情況的發展都會直接地或間接地被它的環境影響；所以一個環境變成構成一個情況的根本因素。

小結

心靈、行動、和一個特定的環境是構成任何情況不可或缺的三個因素，所以戰略無時時刻都必須面對這三個因素。因此，戰略以這三個因素為中心發展出它自己的概念，這些因素變成建立任何戰略思想的重要支柱。於是，這三個因素變成戰略的必要要素。

第二章

戰略的本質

心靈、行動、環境是戰略的根本要素。這三個要素根本地構成戰略，所以戰略的本質必定與這三個要素有很強的關聯性。如果這些要素能被充分地理解，就能更進一步地了解戰略。

心靈

心靈是用來思考的

心靈就是天生設計來思考事情的，每個想法都是在心靈裡面建構和處理而成。構成心靈的事物都是創造想法的原料，同時也是影響思考方式的因素。例如，經驗、感知、知識、價值觀、認知、情緒都是構成心靈的重要成分；這些成分建構任何人的心理本質。這些心理成分是思想的源頭：它們被心靈用來作為創造想法的重要材料。此外，這些成分也是建立心靈的精神結構的基礎原料，這個結構塑造心靈思考的方式。

思考環境的心理能力

心靈的一個重要思考能力就是去研究環境，特別是去研究與人類行動或生活有關的環境。為了瞭解一個環境，心靈從這個環境中搜尋和分析無數的現象或有意義的線索。了解一個環境的進一步目的是藉由知道人類如何被這個環境影響、人類如何與這個環境互動、人類可以在這個環境中做什麼、以及這個環境可能會如何影響人類去評估這個環境與人類之間的關係。一旦心靈清楚了解這個關係，心靈將思考它是否滿意這個關係；然後根據心靈自身的期望，它會考慮透過影響這個環境以調整這個關係。

在思考一個環境的過程中，有關這個環境的實際資訊不是心靈唯一考慮的事物，心靈的心理成份也包含在思考中。所以人類對於一個環境的了解和判斷會受到心靈的心理成份影響。人類對一個環境的了解和判斷影響人類與這個環境的互動方式；這種理解和判斷直接影響人類的行動，並間接地透過人類的行動影響這個環境。

做決定的心理能力

心靈的另外一個思考能力是去做決定。人類希望達成全部他們想要的事物。然而，在有限的精力、時間、資源下，人們只能試著追求少數的願望。因此確定什麼事物是人們想要優先達成的是很重要的。藉著衡量一個人的心理成分、關於環境的資訊、還有其他因素，心靈會將一個人的所有期望排定優先順序、選擇其中一個期望作為最重要的目標、並決定以怎樣的行動或計畫實現這個目標。因此，人類的決策由人類的心靈控制並且受心靈中的心理成份影響。此外，心靈的決定會成為引導人未來如何行動的精神指標。

行動

行動與心靈的相互關係

行動並不會在沒有目的的情況下自動發生，行動是被有意地實施。行動是為了人類的目的被人類心靈的思考程序考慮、選擇、採用。因此，選擇怎樣的行動以及如何實施這個行動都與人們的思考方式有關。

同時，人類實行的任何行動都會影響心靈。實施行動的經驗形成一種回饋去刺激心靈。心靈會參考這個實施經驗重新檢視它的想法並且調整它的思考方式，而這個調整將改變未來行動的選擇和實施。

行動重要的功能

只有透過行動，人類才能實際接觸並處理這個世界上不同種類的事物。為了人類的目的，行動最重要的功能就是透過與一個環境所包含的事物互動去實際地影響這個環境。在與一個環境中的各種事物互動時，行動會根據人類的想法和想像在這個環境中協調整合這些事物去發展一個情況；其結果是，這個環境被行動影響而改變。

環境

任何環境的四個面向

任何環境都有四個面向：物質面向、精神面向、時間、以及空間。這四個面向是塑造每個環境的基本向度。在這個世界上所有的事物都被這四個面向組成或者與這四個面向有關。

-- 物質面向 --

大部分組成這個世界的自然事物都是物質性的，例如植物、地形、海洋、以及空氣。這些自然事物根據自然法則彼此互動。這些自然事物的互動建構出任何環境的物理特性：地理條件、氣候條件、以及生態條件。一個環境的物理特性影響在這個環境中的所有種類事物。

為了在一個環境中生存並且發展生活，人類必須處理任何環境的物理特性。人類一出生並無擁有任何東西只有自己的身體，所以人類探索並利用一個環境存在的任何事物去改變這個環境以改善生活條件並且建立他們的社會。人們利用可取得的天然材料去發明有用的工具、科技、以及其他人造的物品；這些人類發明創造出的物品強化人類與這個世界各種事物的互動能力和影響這些事物的能力。藉由這些人類發明創造的物品的幫助，人類可以更有效率地改變許多環境並且在這些環境發展他們的社會。

此外，許多被人類製造出或建造出的人造事物都融入這個世界成為這個世界的一部份，並且如同自然物質一樣影響這個世界。例如，一個地區的巨大河流會影響這個地區的生態系統。這個河流提供水資源滋養這個地區的動物和植物，為許多生物創造合適的生存條件。如果一個大水壩蓋在這條河流上，這個水壩將減少河流的水流量，而這個地區的生態系統會遭受衝擊。

因此，物質性事物，包含自然的事物和人造的事物，成為了這個世界不可或缺的一部份。這些物質性事物根本地建構任何環境並且重大地影響任何環境。人類承受物質性事物的影響，但也為了生活和建立社會仰賴物質性的事物。總之，物質性事物基本上構成每個環境重要的一個面向。

-- 精神面向 --

物質性事物不是塑造和影響任何環境的唯一因素，人類本身也是重要的因素。人類受他們的想法和思考方式影響。人類根據他們如何考慮將自身的生活改善，去影響一個環境的物理特性。有些人偏好融入一個地區的生態系統而不去大規模的改變這個生態系統。為了自己方便，有些人喜好藉著改變地形和管理動物及植物以控制一個區域的生態系統。為了社會的長久發展，許多人透過大規模地在地上和地下放置大型人工建物去改變許多地區的地理條件。

除了塑造任何環境物質性的一面，人們也思考如何與其他人互動。所有人類都為了他們的目的試著影響世界的任何事物，特別是影響其他人；因此，任何人都有可能影響另外一個人或者被另外一個人影響。每個人都會思考應該採取怎樣的行動去影響其他人或處理其他人的行動。而一個人的想法會影響這個人如何採取行動與其他人互動。

採取行動並非唯一影響其他人的方式。人類將他們的想法轉變成許多不同的文化或社會要素，例如語言、藝術、法律、社會制度、組織、教育、宗教、傳統、社會價值、等等…。當人們與這些要素互動並且將這些要素納入思考時，構成這些要素的想法就會影響人們的行為和思考。因此，人們可以透過這些社會和文化要素間接地、更大規模地、更長時間地在心理上影響其他人。

無論人類做了什麼去塑造這個世界以及影響其他人，在任何行動和任何決定背後的重要影響因素就是人類的想法。雖然人類的想法本身是看不見的，但人的想法確實以各種不同無形和有形的形式存在著：想法以記憶、經驗、知識、和人格的形式儲存於心靈中；想法影藏在語言、文字、符號、和其他人類創造的事物中；或者想法被轉變成不同的文化和社會系統。這些形式都可被稱之為精神形式因為人類的想法是這些形式本質上的一部份。人類的想法經常透過這些精神形式影響人們如何思考和行動，成為了人類社會中許多事件和情況發生的深層因素。所以當人們遇到其他人和這些人的社會時，人必須將這些精神形式和構成這些形式的想法納入思考。因此，精神性事物，包含各種想法和這些想法存在的形式，構成任何環境重要的一個面向。

-- 時間 --

每個事物都發生在一段特定的時間內並且與自己的歷史時代有深厚的關聯性。每段時間都有自己特殊的歷史情境。任何事物必定以某種方式與它的時代背景有所互動：

某些事物是被與它自己的時代有關的因素造成的；某些事物也許本身就是影響它自己的歷史時期的重要因素；或者某些事物和它的歷史背景相互影響。

此外，任何環境都隨著時間不斷地變化。任何環境都是由它的過去情況發展而來，而這個環境現在的情況正在朝著未來不斷地發展改變。世界上的各種因素將會影響任何環境並且逐漸改變任何環境現在的情況，使得各種環境未來的情況變得與現在的情況大不相同；一個環境的過去情況和現在情況之間的關係也是如此。換句話說，過去造成現在，現在塑造未來。

因為每個環境都不斷地變化，所以任何環境的情況發展都有連續性。過去的因素造成現在的情況，而有些過去的因素仍然融合在現在的情況中保持它們的影響力，例如文化價值和社會系統。同樣地，現在的因素將塑造未來的情況，而且它們的影響力在某種程度上在未來仍會延續下去。所以過去、現在、未來三者彼此相關。

因此，每個環境的一切事物都與時間有關；在這個世界上，各種事物之間彼此建立起時間上的關聯性。知道一個事物屬於什麼歷史時代，就可以去研究這個事物如何被它時代的情境影響以及這個事物如何影響它時代的情境。此外，了解一個情況發生在什麼歷史時期，就能去研究這個情況與它前一個時代的情況之間的關係以及這個情況和它後來時代的情況之間的關係。還有，因為任何環境的情況發展都有連續性，人們可以根據一個環境現在的情況評估這個環境的情況未來的發展。

簡而言之，無論一個事物發生在怎樣的環境中，時間是連結不同歷史時期的情況的重要要素；時間也是將世界上的不同事物彼此連結在一起的關鍵要素。所以，時間是每個環境不可或缺的一個面向。

-- 空間 --

任何環境都是一個實際的空間。無論是物質性還是非物質性，每個事物只要存在一個環境中、與這個環境互動、或者影響這個環境就是在空間上與這個環境有關連性。

空間上，不同種類的事物如何分布在一個環境中以及它們之間的關聯性如何意味著一個環境如何被塑造。如果一種事物普遍分布在一個環境大部分的區域中，這個事物就構成這個環境的基本特色。如果這種事物不只普遍分布在這個環境中，這種事物的存在性和影響力還勝過其他種類的事物，明顯地這種事物主宰這個環境的特性。在另外一例子中，有許多種類的事物都普遍分布於一個環境中，但任何一種事物都無法壓過其他種類的事物，多樣性就變成這個環境的典型特色。如果一種特定的事物只普遍出現在這世界上的某個地方，這種事物必定變成這個地方的獨特特徵。

此外，任何環境的情況發展也與空間有關。假設一個環境中的任何事物都不會被外界的事物影響，那麼這個環境的情況發展就只會與這個環境本身的因素有關；然而，如果這個環境發生的事情經常與鄰近地區的許多事物相互關聯，這個環境的情況就容易受到鄰近地區（因素）的影響。如果遙遠地方所發生的事情經常與一個環境的情況互相影響，這個環境的情況發展在某種長度上就與遙遠地區的因素有關。

如同任何環境的情況，任何因素也與空間有關。一個因素可以與許多遙遠地方所發生的事情互動，這因素就能夠跨區域地影響許多環境。如果，另外一個因素可以同時在一個廣大的範圍內和無數不同種類的事物互動，這個因素就可能會造成大規模發生的情況。

因此世界上的每種事物都與空間有關，因為每個環境都是一個實際的空間。如果沒有將空間規模納入思考，任何環境情況的發展、各種事物間的互動、以及不同因素的影響力都無法完整地解釋。簡單地說，空間是每個環境的一個重要面向。

環境是行動的背景

任何環境都是行動實施的背景；每個環境都提供行動

所需的資源。為了根據人們的想法影響一個環境，實施行動是必要的。然而，人類自身的力量是有限的，所以人們利用在一個環境中所找到的事物去強化他們的行動。例如，人類採集一個地方的金屬礦並將礦石打造成不同種類的金屬工具，這些工具能強而有力地幫助人改變這個地方的地理景觀。此外，在歷史上，藉由利用文化和社會系統，居住在一個區域中的人們經常將他們自己整合成一個強而有力的社群以對抗鄰近的軍事敵人，或者他們建立一個互相合作的社群一起在他們生活區域建造和管理大規模的水利系統以發展農業。無論一個環境的資源是物質性的還是精神性的，它們都被人類利用來強化行動以影響這個環境。

任何環境不只是一個包含各種資源給行動使用的地方，同時也是影響行動的背景。每個環境都包含各種不同的因素，這些因素之間的互動構成一個環境的基本特性，例如：氣候、地形、植物、動物是建構一個環境自然特性的因素；同時，文化價值、宗教傳統、社會系統、經濟發展、政治制度是塑造一個環境社會特性的因素。一個環境的基本特性和因素會影響行動：當一種行動在一個環境中實施時，這個行動會接觸這個環境的因素並與這些因素互動：在互動時，這些因素以及這個環境的特性就會影響這個行動的實施。

環境是心靈的背景

任何環境不只是行動的背景，也是心靈的背景。當心靈蒐集有關一個環境的資訊時，心靈就會使用這個資訊去評估它的想法和思考方式是否真的能幫助人們了解這個環境並且與這個環境互動。如果評估的結果是否定的，心靈將會調整它自己的思考方式。換句話說，一個環境的情況刺激心靈去重新評估和重新調整它自己。因此，環境是影響心靈內部發展的外部背景。

小結

心靈、行動、和環境是構成戰略的根本要素；戰略的本質就是這三個要素之間的互動性關係。心靈是戰略的核心，它建立了行動的概念基礎：心靈發展思想去塑造行動；設定目標去指引行動；並決定實施行動的方式。行動是戰略的催化劑：行動試著將心靈的想法在一個環境中實際實現。環境是戰略的背景：心靈的想法在這個背景中發展出來，而這個背景也是行動實施的地方。

這三個戰略要素之間的關係並不是單向的，而是雙向的。心靈決定如何實施行動以及為何實施行動，同時行動將實施經驗回饋給心靈，促使心靈重新考慮自己的決定和想法。行動影響並且改變一個環境，同時反過來這個環境提供資源給行動並且影響行動的實施。當心靈試著了解一個環境並且計畫去影響這個環境時，這個環境也刺激心靈想法的轉變。

簡而言之，心靈、行動、和環境之間是互相關聯的，這三個要素之間的相互關係建構戰略的本質。

第三章

理解

在研究戰略的本質後，如何應用戰略去達成目的是另外一個令人好奇的問題。然而，無論人們要追求什麼目的，他們都必須面對與這個目的有關的某個環境；為了在這個環境中實現他們的目的，他們必須跟這個環境的情況互動。如果完整地理解這個環境的情況，人們就能設計出一個合適的計畫去處理這個情況以增加達成目的的成功機率。因此，無論戰略如何應用在人們的目的上，理解是戰略不可或缺的一個步驟。

理解的基本原則

有關理解，一些有幫助的原則是應該被考慮的。

什麼是真實的取決於真相本身

理解的基本目的就是去找到有關一個情況或是某個事物的真相。人們只有知道一個事物的本質或是到底真正發生什麼情況，他們才能為了這個事物或情況制定合適的計畫。

人類通常透過他們已經學到的事物去尋找真相：許多人依賴經驗、知識、理論去尋找什麼才是真實的。人們相信這些被組織而成的思想概念（經驗、知識、理論）能真的告訴他們什麼才是真相並且引導他們辨認什麼才是真實的。然而，這些思想概念所教導人們的東西是完全不一樣的，這些概念只是根據過去研究出的事物告訴人們一個情況可能會是怎樣或者哪些因素之間可能彼此相關。

經驗、知識、理論在理解的過程中的角色是提示可能的線索以及刺激人們去調查可能和真相有關的事物，而非直接判斷真相是什麼。經驗、知識、理論並不能取代真相因為它們並非真相本身。

比較糟的是，有些人會根據他們個人的價值觀去做研究。個人價值觀只會引導人們尋找他們相信是真實的事物並且迴避他們認為不是真實的事物。因此，這些人所理解到的只是符合他們價值觀標準的資訊，而不是真相。

什麼是真實的只能由真相本身決定。理解真相的基本方式就是去尋找和證明一個事物的根本性質還有到底真正發生什麼事情，而不是只根據所學的事物和個人價值觀直接下結論。

察覺世界的複雜性

真實世界是複雜的。世界上的許多情況都是由各種因素塑造而成的；這些因素的多樣性以及它們之間的關係的多樣性使許多情況變得複雜。因為這樣的多樣性，幾乎不可能將所有的因素納入考慮。所以完全地了解一個情況是困難的。

因為一個情況的複雜性，知道完整地理解這個情況是困難的，所以簡化這個情況成為了一個替代方式，因為研究一個簡化的情況是較為容易的。簡化的方式是去尋找造成一個情況的重要因素並且分析這些因素是如何造成這個情況。然而，「簡化一個情況」這個概念有時被誤用，人們有時只選擇少數幾個因素去解釋一個情況。「簡化」的概念是去尋找真正塑造一個情況的重要因素，而不將太多無關的因素和不重要的因素納入考慮。「簡化」的目的是理解一個情況，同時不使心靈思考太多細節，而非只是減少因素的數量。過度簡化不只忽略不重要的因素，也忽略掉一些重要的因素，減少了基本地理解一個情況的可能性。

因此，嘗試理解任何事物時，同時察覺世界的複雜性是必要的。這種對複雜性的察覺力提醒人們去思考在研究一個情況時是否將這個情況過度簡化。

任何情況都隨時會變化

任何情況都不會永遠不變，而是隨著時間持續改變。一個情況在被研究之後多少會有所改變，所以不要過度依賴已經研究出的資訊是很重要的。任何情況的情報都應該隨時保持更新。

如何開始理解一個情況

去尋找什麼事物以及什麼人是有關聯的

在討論完上述三個原則後，如何開始理解一個情況是下一個令人關心的議題。因為戰略是由心靈、行動、和環境建構而成，理解一個情況就從這三個戰略要素開始。第一步驟是從這三個戰略要素的角度去尋找與一個情況有重大關聯性的事物和人；什麼事物以及什麼人是有關連的是以這些事物和人是否會影響一個情況或者被這個情況影響所定義的。為了尋找什麼事物以及什麼人是有關連的可以從思考幾個問題開始，例如：

人類和他們的心靈

- 誰重大地影響或造成某一個情況？
- 誰被某個情況嚴重地影響？
- 誰想要去影響某一個情況？
- 誰將影響某一個情況？
- 誰將被某一個情況影響？
- 這些影響情況的人或將會影響情況的人的想法和思考方式是什麼？
- 受某個情況影響的人是如何思考的？

環境

- 哪種環境影響某個情況的發展，例如：自然環境、政治環境、經濟環境、社會環境、文化環境、還是其他種類的環境？
- 哪個環境被某一個情況影響？
- 哪種環境將影響某一個情況？
- 哪種環境將被某個情況影響？
- 哪種環境因素影響某個情況，例如氣候條件、地理條件、軍事衝突、經濟發展、社會系統、文化價值、政治意識形態、或是其他因素？
- 影響某一個情況的環境的空間規模如何？
- 某個情況和它的影響力所包含的地理範圍有多廣？
- 某個情況經歷過什麼歷史年代？
- 什麼樣的歷史因素和歷史情境造成某一個情況的發展？

行動

- 什麼樣的人類行動造成某一個情況的發生？
- 什麼樣的行動被某一個情況影響？
- 什麼樣的行動將造成某一個情況？
- 什麼樣的行動將被某一個情況影響？
- 被某一個情況影響的人將會採取什麼行動處理這個情況？

透過這些問題的幫助，就有可能找到有關聯的人和事物。

研究有關聯的人和事物

知道什麼人以及什麼事物是有關聯的之後，下一個步驟就是去研究這些人和事物。首先要研究的是這些人和事物的本質。本質至少由兩種成分構成：第一種成分是構成一個事物或一個人的基本性質，而這個性質會無時無刻影響一個事物或一個人；另外一種成分是造成這個基本性質的根本原因。因此，研究任何事物的本質可以先分析它的基本性質然後調查造成這個性質的原因。例如，一個人的基本性質就是這個人的想法和思考方式，因為一個人在思考什麼以及如何思考都不斷地影響這個人的行為。塑造一個人想法和思考方式的其中一個重要因素就是這個人心理特質；這個人心靈的心理成分建構了這個人的心理特質。

下一個研究的重點是調查這些有關聯的人事物之間的關係。調查的重要任務在於去了解這些有關聯的人事物之間的因果關係：什麼事物或什麼人影響了哪個事物或哪個人；造成影響的（人事物）如何與被影響的（人事物）互動；他們（造成影響的以及被影響的人事物）之間的互動造成了什麼結果。

藉由研究與一個情況有關聯的人事物的本質以及他們之間的關係，人們就能基本理解這個情況：人們能清楚分析出到底已經發生了什麼、正在發生什麼、以及這個情況如何被造成的。

預測

依據對一個情況的研究，以及對一個情況有關的人事物的分析，這個情況將會如何發展或者什麼事情將會發生都可以被合理地預測。例如：人們將會採取什麼行動去改變這個情況？環境因素將會如何改變這個情況？一個情況將會如何影響某個環境？

對一個情況有深入的了解並且對這個情況有合理的預測，人就可以設計出一個合適的計畫去處理這個情況。

第四章

規劃

除了理解，規劃是戰略的另一個重要步驟。為了提升達成目標的機率，一個計劃的基本功能就是思考如何去管理人所能做的事還有如何去管理人所能利用的事物以面對已經發生的事情、現在正在發生的事情、以及未來將會發生的事情。在沒有思考和缺乏準備之下任意地實施行動將會浪費自己擁有的事物以及破壞自己所做的事情，並且危害達成目標的可能性。這也是為什麼人類經常會制定計畫的原因。

以下將討論一些概念，這些概念對於規劃是有用的指引。

去思考計畫的整體結果

「達到目標就是好的結果」是很常見的想法。然而，如果目標的達成是以失去所有東西換來的，這樣的結果是好的嗎？如果一個計劃實現了，但這個計畫的實行卻造成了會對未來情況不利的副作用，這個結果可以被視為好的結果嗎？這兩個問題的答案必定是否定的，所以重新思考什麼結果才是好的相當重要。

無論一個計劃想要達成什麼目的，這個計畫造成的整體結果是這個計畫無可避免將會面對的：一個計劃的目標是否會達成只是結果的一部份；這個計劃的實行會如何影響當前的情況也包括在結果內。除了達成目標，如果一個計劃對當前情況造成的影響是有益的或者至少不太有害，那麼整體結果就會變得更好。因此，將整體結果納入考量，而非只思考它本身的目的。至少人們能做的就是去思考一個計劃的實行或者是一個計劃的行動有可能會造成什麼影響（或後果）。

簡而言之，只有實現目的對一個計劃還不夠好，在達成目的之外還能產生良好的整體結果才是更好的。

思考對計劃有正面幫助的事物以及不利的事物

正面幫助的事物

有關設計計畫的一個概念就是去找到對一個計畫有正

面幫助的或是將會有正面幫助的任何事物，以增加這個計劃成功的可能性。對於這個概念，思考什麼事物對一個計劃是有利的是一個可行的方式。例如：哪一個思想、技能、資源對促進一個計畫的實施是確實有用的；我們擁有怎樣的資源、知識、或其他有利的事物可以強化我們實現計畫目標的能力；那些環境因素對於幫助一個計劃的實行是有價值的？找到對一個計劃有利的事物將會更方便地推動這個計畫的實行。

另外一個方式是去找到機會，例如：什麼時候才是實施某種行動的合適時間點；還有什麼可能的方法可以用來幫助實行一個計劃；還有任何未發現但可以利用的環境因素或資源嗎？去尋找機會就是去了解什麼事物對於進一步推動一個計劃的實行是有潛在幫助的。

第三個可行的方式就是去發展對一個計劃將有正面幫助的事物。人們可以創造或發展他們所缺乏的事物如果他們認為這個事物對於實現他們的目的將會是必要的而且有幫助的，而不是過度依賴他們現在所擁有的事物。例如：一個國家可以培養它所沒有的某種產業如果這種產業對於這個國家的經濟發展是有幫助的。去發展將會有正面幫助的事物就是為了一個計劃改善當前的情況。因此，規劃不應該只是思考當前的情況是如何，還要考慮如何改善目前的情況以幫助一個計劃的實行。除了人們現在所擁有的事物，如果他們缺乏某些事物，而這些事物將對一個計劃是有幫助的，人們就可以為了這個計畫去發展這些事物。

不利的事物

為了對有可能會妨礙或危害一個計劃的事物有所準備，尋找現在會或將來對這個計畫不利的任何事物是另一個規劃的必要概念。跟這個概念有關的一個方式是去檢視一個計劃本身的限制性，例如：這個計畫有多少資源可以使用；這個計畫的時間限制為何；實行這個計畫的組織的最大力量是什麼？藉由了解一個計畫的限制性，就可以清楚地知道這個計畫能做什麼、不能做什麼；然後這個計畫才可以謹慎的管理它的行動和資源。此外，一個計畫也才不會去過度利用各種事物而超出這些事物的限度。

另外一個方式就是去考慮成本。每個事物都需要花費某種程度的努力、時間、資源才能良好地運作或者被成功地發展；一個計畫的實施當然也花費某些事物。一個計畫到底需要多少時間和資源？一個計畫需要怎樣的技能和專業能力？何種行動對某個計畫而言是必要的？藉著了解一個計畫的成本以及它的限制性，就可以評估這個計畫可以做什麼、不可以做什麼；這個計畫才能因此有效率地及合理地調節它的資源和行動。

除了了解計畫的限制性和成本，另外一個方式是去研究有可能會對一個計劃造成危害的事物，例如：誰將會妨礙這個計畫的實施；哪個環境因素會對這個計畫的實施造成有害的影響；哪種妨礙計畫實行的突發狀況會發生？研究什麼事物會危害一個計畫的目的就是為了這個計畫做好準備以消除或減弱任何風險。

世界上各種因素以不同的方式影響一個計畫。因此考慮有可能會影響實現一個計畫的可能性的不同因素對規劃而言是重要的；至少應該要去調查那些因素對這個計畫是好的還是不好的。

全盤性地思考

在這個世界上，不同的事物或因素透過互動彼此連結一起，例如，國內政治、國際政治、軍事能力、經濟發展、和貿易之間彼此的相互關係；它們透過一種連鎖反應的方式彼此直接地或間接地彼此互相影響，這種連鎖反應的方式是因素之間的一個互動會觸發另一個互動。其結果是，不同的事物建構出一個相互連結的系統，在這個系統中系統的任何成員都會彼此相互影響。此外，所有的成員藉由它們之間的互動共同發展出這個系統的性質，而這個系統的性質與個別成員的性質大不相同。在這個系統裡面或者是進入這個系統的任何事物都會遭受這個系統的性質和成員的影響。

每個情況都是一個由許多不同因素構成的系統。在一個情況中的不同因素並非彼此獨立而是相互有關聯的。這些因素之間的互動發展、維持、以及轉變這個情況。換句話說，一個情況是建立在這個情況不同因素之間的整體相互關係上。當一個計畫想要了解任何情況時，這個計畫必須研究這個情況不同因素之間的整體相互關係，而非只是個別的分析不同的因素。因此，為了面對任何情況，全盤性的思考方式對一個計畫是必要的。

此外，可以用整體的角度觀察一個計畫：一個計劃是一個有組織性的結構，而非只是由許多不同想法隨意拼裝而成的東西。如果一個計畫是一個結構，這個計畫的目的和一些原則就組成這個結構的核心，這個核心是這個計畫設計的依據。行動和不同的實施方式是支撐核心的主要支柱，它們的主要功能就是執行這個計畫的想法以達成目的。管理資源以及協調資源和行動是這個結構的基礎，這個基礎協助計畫的實施。這個計畫其餘的部分是用來支援執行行動、管理資源、或是其他主要的功能。一個計畫的每個部份彼此相互連結，而所有的部分彼此互相支援。

因此，在規劃時，一個計畫應該被當作一個整合而成的系統，與一個計畫有關的所有事項應該被當作一個整體。組成一個計畫的所有部分都要根據這個計畫想要追求的目的還有一些指導原則去設計。所有的部分都要被系統化以在計畫中擔任不同的功能，而所有的部分都要被安排去支援彼此。

保持心靈的主動和敏感性

因為一個計畫遇到的每個情況都不斷隨著時間變化，心靈必須對一個情況的發展保持敏感度並且主動更新有關這個情況的情報。然後，參考這個更新的情報，應該將心靈原本的計畫重新檢查並修正。

換句話說，心靈不應該在制定一個計畫後就停止思考。任何計畫都不是完美的，也不會總是適當的，所以心靈必須持續注意當前的情況如何以及當前的情況將會如何發展以重新檢視和改善它的計畫。

根據事實思考

如果確實地了解一個情況，一個計畫就可以用適合的方式處理這個情況。因此，一個計畫必須根據事實思考，而非只是根據猜測和想像。雖然一個計畫可能包含假設、建議、和預測，這些想法也必須根基於實際的情況思考而成。

第五章

重新檢視心靈

以戰略而言，無論選擇何種行動、產生何種想法、一個計畫怎樣被設計出來，心靈都深切地影響有關這些事物的思考；所以嚴格地重新檢視心靈是重要的。

首先，心靈正在思考什麼應該被清楚地調查出來。然後，還要研究哪些因素影響心靈的思考，以及這些因素如何影響心靈的思考。如此，就可以大概了解心靈在思考什麼、以什麼方式思考。

下一個步驟是根據邏輯、真相、還有其他合理的依據去測試心靈的想法和思考方式的合理性和可靠性。這個目的是為了檢驗心靈的想法和思考方式對於研究能力、判斷能力、分析能力、以及規畫能力是否有幫助或是不利。

第三個步驟是調整心靈的想法和思考方式。

還有，最好是能經常嚴格地練習研究、分析、仔細思考、以及判斷各種情況去提升心靈的思考能力。

戰略從心靈開始。一旦人們想要了解這個世界並且在這個世界追求他們的目的，與戰略相關的想法就會從他們的心中產生。而這個想法會重大地影響思考、規劃、還有計畫的實施。因此，察覺、評估、並且改善心靈的想法和思考方式是很重要的。

版權頁

書名：To Explore Strategy 探索戰略
語言：Bilingual Edition(中英雙語版)
版本：初版
作者：Chong Han Wang(王崇翰)
編輯：Chong Han Wang(王崇翰)
出版者：Chong Han Wang(王崇翰)
地址：950 台灣台東市青海路四段 400 號
Email：worldjody@gmail.com
電話：089-510090
出版：2016 年 11 月

國家圖書館出版品預行編目 (CIP) 資料

探索戰略 / 王崇翰著 . -- 初版 . -- 臺東市 : 王崇翰 , 2016.11
面； 公分
中英對照
ISBN 978-957-43-3955-6(平裝)

1. 戰略 2. 戰略思想

592 105017656

ISBN 978-957-43-3955-6 平裝
ISBN 978-957-43-3976-1 電子書 (PDF)

www.ingramcontent.com/pod-product-compliance
Ingram Content Group UK Ltd.
Pitfield, Milton Keynes, MK11 3LW, UK
UKHW021654190726
13853UKWH00001B/248